50 Fill-In Math Word Problems

MULTIPLICATION & DIVISION

Grades 4–6

by Bob Krech and Joan Novelli

SCHOLASTIC

New York • Toronto • London • Auckland • Sydney
Mexico City • New Delhi • Hong Kong • Buenos Aires

Teaching Resources

Thanks to Andrew and Faith for laughing

Editor: Joan Novelli
Cover design by Ka-yeon Kim
Interior design by Holly Grundon
Interior illustrations by Mike Moran

ISBN-13: 978-0-545-07485-8
ISBN-10: 0-545-07485-1

Copyright © 2009 by Bob Krech and Joan Novelli.
Illustrations © 2009 by Scholastic Inc.
All rights reserved.
Printed in the U.S.A.
Published by Scholastic Inc.

1 2 3 4 5 6 7 8 9 10   40   15 14 13 12 11 10 09

Contents

Fill-In Math Word Problems

About This Book

When we learn to read, we learn to recognize the letters of the alphabet, we practice letter-sound relationships, and we learn punctuation, but what it's all about is eventually being able to read text. A similar situation exists in math. We learn to recognize and write numerals, what the symbols mean, and we learn operations like multiplication and division, but what it's all about is what you can do with these skills—applying what you know to solve problems. *50 Fill-In Math Word Problems: Multiplication & Division* provides lots of funny stories to fill in—and some very interesting problems to solve.

What Are Fill-In Math Word Problems?

A fill-in math word problem is a funny story with a math problem waiting to happen. Most of the word problem is already supplied except for a few key words and numbers that have been removed and replaced with blanks. It's up to the students to fill in those blanks with missing nouns, verbs, adjectives, and other types of words—just like in some other popular word games. The difference is that this game is missing some numbers as well. When your students supply the missing numbers along with the words, they suddenly have a wacky, math word problem that's fun to read and solve!

Why Use Fill-In Math Word Problems?

Traditional math word problems can provide a meaningful context for students to apply their skills, but sometimes the problems can be a bit boring. Remember trying to figure out when the two trains would pass each other? That won't happen with *50 Fill-In Math Word Problems*. Students help create these wacky word problems, which provide for plenty of good problem-solving practice with grade-appropriate math skills and concepts. Have fun while doing math? Absolutely!

Teaching With Fill-In Math Word Problems

The stories in this book are organized by operation and skill level, beginning with multiplication stories followed by division. You can choose a fill-in story to use with the entire class, or select as many as needed to match different ability levels of students. For instance, you might have some students who would benefit from practice with single-digit multiplication, while others may be ready for the challenge of double-digit multiplication. (For connections to the math standards, see Meeting the Math Standards, page 12.) Whatever the need, there is a set of fill-in stories to support it. Following is the order of stories by skills.

- Single-Digit Multiplication
- Single-Digit × Double-Digit Multiplication
- Double-Digit × Double-Digit Multiplication
- Single-Digit × Triple-Digit Multiplication
- Double-Digit × Triple-Digit Multiplication
- Triple-Digit × Triple-Digit Multiplication
- Multiplying Basic Fractions
- Division With Single-Digit Divisor and Single-Digit Dividend
- Division With Single-Digit Divisor and Single- or Double-Digit Dividend

- Division With Single-Digit Divisor and Double-Digit Dividend
- Division With Single-Digit Divisor and Four-Digit Dividend
- Division With Double-Digit Divisor and Triple-Digit Dividend
- Division With Double-Digit Divisor and Four-Digit Dividend
- Dividing Simple Fractions

Teaching Tips

When teaching with the stories in this book, be sure to review and reinforce the following strategies with students.

- When performing operations, align digits properly to avoid mistakes in computation.

- Use commas in numbers with four or more digits to keep all those digits organized.

- When comparing numbers—for example, to see which one is greater—write down the numbers one on top of the other, with the digits aligned, in order to make an accurate visual comparison.

- When solving equations, check the final answer and ask yourself if it makes sense. To do a number-sense check, round the numbers in question for a good, reasonable estimate of what the answer should be. This provides a point of comparison to determine whether the actual answer does indeed make sense. (For more problem-solving strategies, see Teaching Problem-Solving Skills: The Fantastic Five-Step Process, page 9.)

- Remember you can use inverse operations to check computations. For example, it is a good idea to check division computation by multiplying the quotient by the divisor to yield the dividend.

Modeling the Process

Before expecting students to do the stories on their own, model the process of filling in the blanks for a story and solving the problem. Use an overhead to project the story so students can follow along. Invite a student to help you out, and follow these steps:

1. Starting at the beginning of the story, read the prompts for the fill-ins—for instance, "adjective." Write in the adjective your helper suggests—for example, *swirly*.

2. When you have filled in all of the blanks, read aloud the story, beginning with the title.

3. Read aloud the problem in "Solve This!" and think aloud as you use information from the story to solve the problem. (This is a good time to model how to use the Fantastic Five-Step Process. See page 9 for more information.)

How to Fill in the Blanks

Each fill-in math word problem requires students to fill in a set of words and numbers to complete the story. They will then use some of the information they provide to solve the problem. Following is more detailed information about how to fill in the blanks.

Choosing Words

From singular and plural nouns to adverbs and exclamations, different kinds of words are required to fill in the blanks of fill-in math word problems. Review each type of word with students, using the Word Choice Chart (page 13) as a guide. To help students create their own handy references, have them complete the third column of their chart with additional examples of each type of fill-in. They can refer to this when completing stories as a reminder of what kinds of words they can use. You might also consider transferring the descriptions and examples to a wall chart for easy reference.

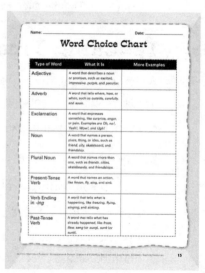

Note that, at times, students will also have to fill in other types of words, such as a type of instrument, name of an animal, or name of a famous person. These are not included in the chart, as they are already specific enough to support students in their word choice. When you introduce any new story to students, just take a moment to review the different types of words that will be required.

Choosing Numbers

Many stories include fill-ins that give students choice within a range, such as "single-digit number greater than 1." Some fill-ins are more open-ended—for example, "number greater than 1." Other stories may be more specific about the number choice—for example, "choose a number: 2, 3, 4, or 6" in "Driving to the Movies" (page 42). You may choose to let students fill in numbers according to the directions in the stories as is, or you can modify the parameters to provide for differentiation of instruction, individualizing the problems for students by using the number ranges that make sense for them. However, keep in mind that leaving the number size open-ended to some extent is an interesting option and will provide information as to students' ability to work with different-size numbers.

A Note About Remainders

Depending on the numbers students choose as fill-ins for some of the division stories, once the division is done, remainders may result. For example with "Land Rush!" (page 44), space explorers discover land and decide to divide it equally among themselves. Depending on the number of explorers (for example, 8) and acres of land (for example, 57), when students solve the problem and divide, they may be left with a remainder. This is a great opportunity to emphasize number sense and real application of math knowledge. It helps students think about, "How do we quantify remainders in story problems and then, how do we deal with them?" When students begin one of these division stories, make them aware that remainders are possible and emphasize the importance of including that information in their answers, and thinking about what they might do with a remainder in the specific story situation. For example, in solving for the number of acres of land each explorer would get using the numbers above, students might answer that "each explorer gets 7 acres of land, and there would be 1 acre leftover. They could divide that one extra acre among themselves so that each explorer would end up with 7 1/8 acres." This is a sensible way to deal with a remainder in a real context.

Lesson Formats

There are many ways to use the stories in *50 Fill-In Math Word Problems* in your classroom. Suggested lesson formats follow.

1. Problem-Solving Partners

Have students pair up. Make copies of a fill-in story and distribute to one student in each pair. These students are the Readers. Without revealing the title or any parts of the story itself, Readers ask their partners for the missing words and numbers in order ("plural noun," "adjective," "single-digit number greater than 1," and so on) and fill in the appropriate blanks with their partner's responses. When all the blanks are filled in, the Reader reads the completed story. The resulting silly story now contains a math word problem! Partners solve the problem (together or independently), sharing strategies and checking their answers.

2. Class Stories

Choose a story and let students take turns supplying words and numbers to fill in the blanks (again, just read the fill-in prompts in turn, but do not reveal the story at this point). When the story is complete, read it to the class. Have students take notes on the numbers in the story and the problem they need to solve. (Or write this information on chart paper for them.) Students can work together as a class, with a partner, or independently to solve the problem. As a follow-up, let students share answers and discuss problem-solving strategies.

3. Story Switcheroo

After students fill in the blanks for a story with a partner, make copies and distribute to the class for extra practice or homework. Twenty different versions of one story mean 20 different problems to solve! And students will love seeing their work used as a teaching tool!

4. Math Practice Pages

Invite pairs of students to create stories for a binder full of practice pages. They fill in the stories as described in "Problem-Solving Partners" (see above), but solve the problem and write an explanation on the back of the paper. For extra practice, students can take a story from the binder, solve the problem (on a separate sheet of paper), and check their answer on the back. They can then return the story to the binder.

5. Create New Stories

Creating new fill-in stories is another option for practicing math skills—and a motivating way to connect writing and math. Using the stories in this book as models, invite students to write their own wacky, fill-in math stories. With students' permission, copy the stories and distribute to the class for homework (or in-class practice). Guide students in following these steps to create their stories.

- Identify a skill area and write this at the top of the paper. You may choose to specify a skill area for students, such as "Single-Digit Multiplication," or leave this up to students to decide.

- Brainstorm story ideas. Everyday events, such as doing chores or baking cupcakes, can make for very funny stories. Think about how multiplication or division might fit into the story. For example, if you're saving up for something, and you get paid three dollars every week for taking out the trash, multiplication is a quick way to figure out how much you'll have in a month.

- Write a draft of your story. Do not try to make your story "funny." Just write about the event as if you were telling someone else about it. When you're finished, underline some of the verbs, adjectives, nouns, and numbers, then erase the original word. Label the type of word or number beneath each blank. Be sure to set up a math problem in the story.

- Write the problem to be solved in the space labeled "Solve This!" Solve the problem yourself to make sure it works.

- Draw a picture to illustrate the story.

Teaching Problem-Solving Skills:

The Fantastic Five-Step Process

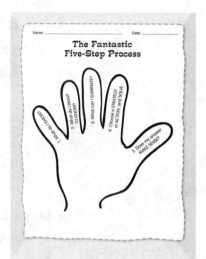

Problem solving is the first process standard listed in the National Council of Teachers Mathematics (NCTM) *Principles and Standards for Mathematics*. The accompanying statement reads, "Problem solving is an integral part of all mathematics learning. In everyday life and in the workplace, being able to solve problems can lead to great advantages. However, solving problems is not only a goal of learning mathematics but also a major means of doing so. Problem solving should not be an isolated part of the curriculum but should involve all Content Standards." In other words, in mathematics, problem solving is what it's all about!

What do you do when you first encounter a math word problem? This is what we need to help students deal with. We need to help them develop a process that they can use effectively to solve any type of math word problem. Word problems often intimidate students because there may be a lot of information, the information is embedded in text, and unlike a regular equation, it is not always clear exactly what you are supposed to do. When using these fill-in math word problems, you may want to take some time to teach (and subsequently review) the Fantastic Five-Step Process for problem solving.

The Fantastic Five-Step Process helps students approach problem solving in a logical, systematic way. No matter what type of problem students encounter, these five steps will help them through it. Learning and using the five steps will help students organize their interpretation and thinking about the problem. This is the key to good problem solving—organizing for action. The best way to help students understand the process is to demonstrate it as you work through a problem on the whiteboard or overhead. Make a copy of the graphic organizer on page 14. You can enlarge this to poster size or provide students with individual copies to follow along as you take them through an introductory lesson.

Step 1: What Do I Know?

Begin by writing the following problem on the chalkboard or overhead:

> Amelia just turned 11 and started her own business selling homemade granola bars. She bought 13 bags of oats to make a giant batch of the most popular bar—the Toasty Oaty Delight. Each bag has 10 cups of oats in it. The recipe for Toasty Oaty Delights calls for 113 cups of oats. Does Amelia have enough cups of oats to make the recipe?

Ask students to read the problem carefully. Ask: "What are the facts?" Have students volunteer these orally. Write them on the board—for example:

- Amelia is 11 years old.
- Amelia started a business selling homemade granola bars.
- Amelia bought 13 bags of oats.
- Toasty Oaty Delight is her most popular granola bar.
- Each bag has 10 cups of oats in it.
- Amelia needs 113 cups of oats to make the recipe.

Encourage students to write down the facts themselves. This will help them focus on what's important while looking for ways to put it in a more accessible form.

Step 2: What Do I Want to Know?

What is the question in the problem? What are we trying to find out? It's a good idea to have students state the question and also determine how the answer will be labeled. For example, if the answer is 72, 72 what? 72 cups? 72 cakes? In this problem we want to know if Amelia has enough cups of oats to make the granola bars. We know she needs 113 cups. We also know she has 13 bags with 10 cups in each bag, but is that at least 113 cups?

Step 3: What Can I Eliminate?

Once we know what we are trying to find out, we can decide what is unimportant. You may need all the information, but often enough there is extra information that can be put aside to help focus on the facts. For example, we can eliminate the fact that Amelia is 11 years old and started a business. We can also ignore Toasty Oaty Delight being the most popular bar. We're left with the following:

- Amelia has 13 bags of oats.
- Each bag has 10 cups of oats in it.
- Amelia needs 113 cups of oats.

Step 4: Choose a Strategy or Action and Solve.

Is there an action in the story—for example, is something being "taken away" or is something being "shared"—that will help us decide on an operation or a way to solve the problem? We have to find out if Amelia has enough oats. We know she has some, but how many cups? In order to know this, we have to find out if 13 bags of 10 cups each is at least 113 cups. We need to multiply the 13 bags by 10 cups in each, and compare the resulting product to 113. When we do the multiplication, we find that 13 x 10 = 130, which is more than 113, and so the answer is "Yes!" Amelia does have enough oats.

Step 5: Does My Answer Make Sense?

Reread the problem. Look at the answer. Is it reasonable? Is it a sensible answer given what we know? The answer does make sense. A quick estimate using the basic fact of 10 x 10, helps us know that our answer of 130 is in the right range. To check a little further, we know that 10 x 10 = 100, and recall that there are actually 13 bags, so 3 extra bags of 10 cups of oats (3 x 10) makes 30 more cups, and 100 + 30 = 130. This is the answer we got when we multiplied, so using this other strategy of breaking the number apart and then adding confirms that our answer is correct.

Try a couple of sample word problems using this "talk-through" format with students. You might invite students to try the problem themselves first and then review step-by-step together, sharing solutions to see if all steps were considered and solutions are in fact correct. Practicing the process in this way helps make it part of a student's way of thinking mathematically.

Teaching Tip

Note that there are no answer keys for the fill-in math word problems as answers will vary depending on the numbers students supply to fill in the blanks. You might set up a buddy system for checking answers or have students turn in their stories for you to check. The fill-in stories provide good opportunities to reinforce strategies for determining if an answer is reasonable.

Meeting the Math Standards

The fill-in math word problems in this book include math content designed to support you in meeting the following math standards for number and operations across grades 4–6, as outlined by the National Council of Teachers of Mathematics (NCTM) in *Principles and Standards for School Mathematics.*

Number and Operations

Understand numbers, ways of representing numbers, relationships among numbers, and number systems

- understand the place-value structure of the base-ten number system and be able to represent and compare whole numbers and decimals
- recognize equivalent representations for the same number and generate them by decomposing and composing numbers
- develop understanding of fractions as parts of unit wholes, as parts of a collection, as locations on number lines, and as divisions of whole numbers

Understand meanings of operations and how they relate to one another

- understand various meanings of multiplication and division
- understand the effects of multiplying and dividing whole numbers
- identify and use relationships between operations, such as division as the inverse of multiplication, to solve problems
- understand and use properties of operations, such as the distributivity of multiplication over addition

Compute fluently and make reasonable estimates

- develop fluency with basic number combinations for multiplication and division and use these combinations to mentally compute related problems
- develop fluency in adding, subtracting, multiplying, and dividing whole numbers
- develop and use strategies to estimate the results of whole-number computations and to judge the reasonableness of such results

- develop and use strategies to estimate computations involving fractions and decimals in situations relevant to students' experience
- select appropriate methods and tools for computing with whole numbers

The word problems in this book also support the NCTM process standards as follows:

Problem Solving

- solve problems that arise in mathematics and other contexts
- apply and adapt a variety of appropriate strategies to solve problems

Reasoning and Proof

- select and use various types of reasoning and methods of proof

Communication

- communicate mathematical thinking coherently and clearly

Connections

- understand how mathematical ideas interconnect and build on one another
- recognize and apply mathematics in contexts outside of mathematics

Representation

- create and use representations to organize, record, and communicate mathematical ideas
- use representations to model and interpret physical, social, and mathematical phenomena

Source: *Principles and Standards for School Mathematics* (National Council of Teachers of Mathematics, 2000-2004); www.standards.nctm.org.

Vocabulary-Building Connections

Take advantage of vocabulary-building opportunities that these fill-in stories present. For example, in the story "Broadway Show" (page 25), students will encounter the word *cuisine.* Use words such as this to spark investigations of word origins. In this case, students will discover that the word is French for "kitchen," and that it is used in English to mean a style of cooking. Encourage students to be on the lookout for other words that are "borrowed" from other languages. Building word knowledge in this way nurtures an interest in language and promotes a stronger vocabulary.

50 Fill-In Math Word Problems: Multiplication & Division: Grades 4–6 © 2009 by Bob Krech and Joan Novelli, Scholastic Teaching Resources

Word Choice Chart

Type of Word	What It Is	More Examples
Adjective	A word that describes a noun or pronoun, such as *excited, impressive, purple,* and *peculiar.*	
Adverb	A word that tells where, how, or when, such as *outside, carefully,* and *soon.*	
Exclamation	A word that expresses something, like surprise, anger, or pain. Examples are *Oh, no!, Yeah!, Wow!,* and *Ugh!*	
Noun	A word that names a person, place, thing, or idea, such as *friend, city, skateboard,* and *friendship.*	
Plural Noun	A word that names more than one, such as *friends, cities, skateboards,* and *friendships.*	
Present-Tense Verb	A word that names an action, like *freeze, fly, sing,* and *sink.*	
Verb Ending in *-ing*	A word that tells what is happening, like *freezing, flying, singing,* and *sinking.*	
Past-Tense Verb	A word that tells what has already happened, like *froze, flew, sang* (or *sung*), *sank* (or *sunk*).	

Name: _____   Date: _____

The Fantastic
Five-Step Process

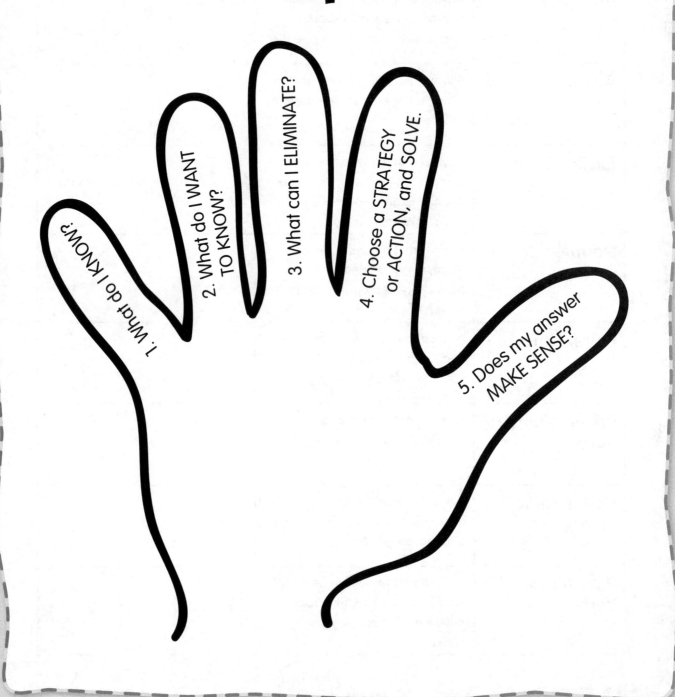

1. What do I KNOW?

2. What do I WANT TO KNOW?

3. What can I ELIMINATE?

4. Choose a STRATEGY or ACTION, and SOLVE.

5. Does my answer MAKE SENSE?

 50 Fill-In Math Word Problems: Multiplication & Division: Grades 4–6 © 2009 by Bob Krech and Joan Novelli, Scholastic Teaching Resources

Name: _____   Date: _____

Donut Day

Our teacher, Ms. _____
(last name of a famous woman)

decided she wanted to have a Donut Day

for our class. She encouraged us to come

to school that day_____
(verb ending in -ed)

like our favorite donuts. _____ of us came as
(single-digit number greater than 1)

_____-flavored donuts. _____
(type of food)   (single-digit number greater than 1)

others came as _____-filled donuts. The teacher gave each
(type of food)

of her _____ lucky students _____
(single-digit number greater than 1)   (single-digit number greater than 1)

special _____ donuts. We saw those donuts and said,
(adjective)

" _____!"
(exclamation)

How many "special donuts" did
the teacher give her students? _____

50 Fill-In Math Word Problems: Multiplication & Division: Grades 4–6 © 2009 by Bob Krech and Joan Novelli, Scholastic Teaching Resources   **15**

Name: _____   Date: _____

Constellations

There are many interesting

constellations in the sky. I like to look at them

through my _____.
                          (noun)

There's the Big _____
                              (noun)

which has _____ stars. Orion's _____
            (single-digit number greater than 1)   (type of clothing)

has _____ stars. The _____
       (single-digit number greater than 1)   (adjective)

_____ constellation has _____
              (noun)   (single-digit number greater than 1)

stars. The newly discovered Galaxy of _____
                                            (last name of a boy or girl)

has _____ constellations, each of which has
       (single-digit number greater than 1)

_____ stars. It is just _____!
(single-digit number greater than 1)   (adjective)

How many stars are in the
newly discovered galaxy? _____

Name: _____   Date: _____

Money From Space

On a recent expedition to Planet

_____, Space
(first name of a boy or girl)

Explorer _____
(first name of a boy or girl)

bought a souvenir _____.
(noun)

It was _____ feet long and _____.
(single-digit number greater than 1)   (color)

Very rare! He paid for it and got _____
(single-digit number greater than 1)

_____-ies back. That's a coin they use on that planet.
(last name of a boy or girl)

Each one of these coins is worth _____ U.S. dollars.
(single-digit number greater than 1)

Our _____ space explorer flew back in his trusty
(adjective)

Starship _____. It only took _____
(last name of a famous person)   (number greater than 1)

minutes. Wow!

Solve This! How many dollars
do the coins equal? _____

Name: _____ Date: _____

Band Uniform

I am in the _____
(name of a school)

Marching Band. I play the _____.
(type of instrument)

I practice _____ hours
(single-digit number greater than 1)

every day. There are _____ band members marching
(single-digit number greater than 1)

in my row. Our favorite song to play is "_____'s
(last name of a boy or girl)

Unfinished Symphony." We just got new band uniforms! They are

_____ and _____ with
(color)   (color)

_____ stripes on the pants. On the front of the jacket,
(color)

there are _____ rows of _____
(single-digit number greater than 1)   (single-digit number greater than 1)

buttons each. The back of the jacket has a picture of a great

_____ _____. Our uniform is so
(verb ending in -ing)   (type of animal)

_____, I even wear it to _____.
(adjective)   (name of a place)

Solve This! How many buttons are there on
the front of a band jacket? _____

Name: _____ Date: _____

New-Style Bowling

_____ Bowlini loves
(first name of a girl)

the new style of bowling. In this style, you

roll a special _____ and
(noun)

try to knock down _____ .
(plural noun)

She played _____ games last _____ .
(single-digit number greater than 1)   (day of the week)

In each game she scored _____ points. She
(choose a number: 10, 20, or 30)

wears a regular _____ on her hand and special
(noun)

_____ . This helps her _____
(footwear)   (present-tense verb)

really well. She also trains by lifting _____ and
(plural noun)

_____ around the track for _____
(verb ending in -ing)   (number greater than 1)

minutes every day. Bowling is not _____ !
(adjective)

How many points did
she score in all? _____

Name: _____ Date: _____

Pay Day!

I have the most _____
(adjective)

job, selling _____ and _____.
(plural noun)   (plural noun)

My boss, Mr. _____, says that when he opened the
(first name of a boy)

store, there were only _____ customers a week.
(number greater than 1)

But his _____ work paid off. Now more than
(adjective)

_____ people shop here each day! As a reward for
(number greater than 1)

shopping with us, every _____ customer gets a free
(ordinal number)

_____! I get paid _____ dollars an
(noun)   (number from 5 to 9)

hour. But that's not all. If I exceed _____ sales in a day, I
(number greater than 1)

get a bonus of _____ _____! This
(number greater than 1)   (plural noun)

week I worked _____ hours. Next week I hope to work
(double-digit number less than 30)

more. Then I know I will get that _____ bonus!
(adjective)

Solve This! How much was the salesperson's
paycheck for the week? _____

Single-Digit × Double-Digit Multiplication

My Life

That incredible Super Star, _____,
                              (first and last name of a boy)

just published his autobiography. It is called *My Life*

and is published by _____ House Publishers. It has
                        (adjective)

ten chapters. Each chapter is _____ pages. The book
                              (single-digit number greater than 1)

tells about how he grew up in _____ and learned to
                              (name of a place)

_____ when he was only _____
    (present-tense verb)   (number greater than 1)

years old. He liked playing with _____ and reading
                                  (plural noun)

books about _____. He had _____
                (plural noun)   (number greater than 1)

sisters and _____ brothers, so they always had to
                (number greater than 1)

share their _____. Soon the book will be made into a
                (plural noun)

movie starring _____. I'm sure it will get really
                (first and last name of a boy)

_____ reviews.
    (adjective)

Solve This! How many pages long is the book? _____

Name: _____ Date: _____

Chip Lover

Have you heard about the Incredible Chip

Contest? I love chips and I was there. It was so

_____! There were all kinds
(adjective)

of different chips to try, including _____ flavored and
(type of food)

_____ flavored. The winner of the contest, though,
(type of food)

was the _____-flavored chip. These chips are so
(type of food)

_____, it's hard to _____ just one.
(adjective)   (present-tense verb)

They come in packages of ten mini-bags. The packaging has a picture of two

_____ eating chips. I love these chips so much I bought
(type of animal, plural)

_____ packages. I can't stop _____
(choose a number: 20, 30, 40, or 50)   (verb ending in -ing)

them. I even eat them while I'm _____.
(verb ending in -ing)

Solve This! How many mini-bags
did the chip lover buy? _____

Name: _____   Date: _____

The Bus

My dad drives a bus. He wears his

_____ _____
(color)   (type of clothing)

and _____ hat. He drives the
(color)

bus from _____ to _____ every day.
(name of a place)   (name of a place)

Last week he drove that route _____ times. The bus holds
(double-digit number)

_____ passengers and it was full every time. He said
(double-digit number)

it got very _____. It costs _____
(adjective)   (single-digit number greater than 1)

dollars for a round-trip ticket. The ride is kind of interesting because you

pass _____ and _____. My dad
(name of a place)   (name of a place)

said that _____ sometimes rides on his bus and so does
(name of a famous person)

_____! The bus is _____ and my
(first and last name of a boy or girl)   (color)

father likes it so much he named it Old _____.
(first name of a boy or girl)

Solve This! How many people rode
the bus last week? _____

Name: _____ Date: _____

My Job

My name is _____.
(first name of a boy)

My job keeps me busy. I _____
(present-tense verb)

_____ in _____.
(plural noun)   (name of a place)

It's not so hard, but I work a lot. Last year I worked _____
(double-digit number)

days and my work day was _____ hours! At least I
(double-digit number less than 25)

don't have to wear _____, the way some people do.
(type of clothing)

My cousin has to _____ _____
(present-tense verb)   (plural noun)

in his job. That is really _____. And he only
(adjective)

gets paid _____ dollars a day. At least I make
(double-digit number)

_____ dollars a day. Plus I get all the _____
(triple-digit number)   (type of food)

I want to eat. You can't beat that!

Solve This! How many hours did
he work last year? _____

Name: _____   Date: _____

Broadway Show

Our class went to see a Broadway show. There were

_____ of us going, so we took a
(double-digit number)

_____ to get there. The ride
(mode of transportation)

there was very _____, but we made it on time.
(adjective)

The show was *Beauty and the* _____, starring
(noun)

_____ and _____. It was
(name of a famous person)   (name of a famous person)

so _____, it was definitely worth the price of the
(adjective)

tickets, which were _____ dollars each. We were
(double-digit number)

_____ all the way through the show. After, we
(verb ending in -ing)

went to a restaurant called The Lucky _____,
(noun)

which serves the traditional cuisine of _____.
(name of a place)

It was a really _____ night.
(adjective)

Solve This! How much did it cost for the
class to see the Broadway show? _____

Name: _____   Date: _____

Exercise Program

There is a new exercise program that is guaranteed

to help you get _____ and
　　　　　　　　　　　　(adjective)

_____. The program is called
　　　　(adjective)

_____-ercise. To start, you have to warm up by running
　　(present-tense verb)

around _____ _____ times. Next
　　　　　(name of a place)　　　　　　　　(number greater than 1)

you lift two _____ over your head _____
　　　　　　　　(plural noun)　　　　　　　　　　　　　　　　(number greater than 1)

times. That helps get your arms _____. Then you take a
　　　　　　　　　　　　　　　　　　　(adjective)

ball and bounce it. You do this _____ times a day, 100
　　　　　　　　　　　　　(single-digit number greater than 1)

bounces each time. Finally, you walk _____ miles carrying a
　　　　　　　　　　　　　　　　(number greater than 1)

big _____ on your _____. Well, it
　　　　(noun)　　　　　　　　　　　　　(body part)

may seem _____, but they say it works.
　　　　　　　(adjective)

How many times do you
bounce the ball in a day? _____

Name: _____   Date: _____

Famous Entertainer

Don't dare miss the next appearance of that

famous entertainer, _____!
_____(first and last name of a girl)

She is going to be appearing at the

_____ for _____ shows only.
(name of a school)   (single-digit number greater than 1)

There will be 100 seats at each show, and each show is sold out. She

will be singing her new hit song, "_____ the
_____(verb ending in -ing)

_____." During her last appearance she wore her favorite
(noun)

_____ _____. The crowd loved it.
(color)   (type of clothing)

They kept calling out, "_____!" She even
(expression)

told a few jokes and then _____ on stage at the end.
(past-tense verb)

It was _____!
(adjective)

How many people will get to
see the famous entertainer? _____

Double-Digit × Triple-Digit Multiplication

Great Product!

_____ had a great idea
(first and last name of a boy)

to make some money. You know he is very

_____ and _____, so he came
(adjective)   (adjective)

up with a super _____ plan. He decided to sell
(adjective)

_____. What an unbelievably _____
(plural noun)   (adjective)

product! Business was great. He sold them at _____
(name of a place)

and at _____ in packs of one hundred. He ended up
(name of a place)

selling _____ packs in _____ days. In
(double-digit number)   (single-digit number greater than 1)

fact, he made _____ dollars! Now he is retired and living in
(number greater than 1)

_____, where he _____
(name of a place)   (verb ending in -s)

all day.

Solve This! How many of the items
were sold altogether? _____

Name: _____   Date: _____

Basketball Star

You probably know _____,
(first and last name of a boy)

the incredible basketball star. He just completed his

_____ basketball career at
(adjective)

_____. He played in 100 games,
(name of a school)

and in every game he scored _____ points.
(double-digit number)

He was so good, his nickname was "The _____."
(noun)

He also set a record for most _____ in a game. That
(plural noun)

was _____. He had an unusual shot, making sure his
(double-digit number)

_____ touched the ball every time. Well, we know for
(body part)

sure he will be very _____ now and everyone will want
(adjective)

his _____!
(noun)

How many points did the basketball
star score in his career? _____

Name: _____ Date: _____

Family Reunion

It's time again for the

_____ family reunion,
(last name of a boy or girl)

and this time _____ people will be there.
(triple-digit number)

My Uncle _____ will be there with his _____
(first name of a boy)   (number greater than 1)

kids. My Aunt _____ will be there, too. She works for a
(first name of a girl)

company that makes _____. We will bring a big picnic
(plural noun)

with lots of _____ and _____.
(type of food)   (type of liquid)

Just for fun, each person will receive _____ lucky tickets for a prize
(double-digit number)

drawing. The grand prize is a brand-new _____!
(noun)

We will also give away ten _____ and a self-propelled
(plural noun)

_____. We always play _____, too.
(noun)   (name of a sport)

It's the most _____ event of the year!
(adjective)

Solve This!

How many lucky tickets will be
given out at the family reunion? _____

50 Fill-In Math Word Problems: Multiplication & Division: Grades 4–6 © 2009 by Bob Krech and Joan Novelli, Scholastic Teaching Resources

Name: _____   Date: _____

Bookmarks

We love reading and

_____ in my class.
(verb ending in *-ing*)

My teacher, Ms. _____, reads books like
(last name of a famous woman)

_____ and *The Revenge of* _____. We
(title of a book)   (first and last name of a boy or girl)

like to listen to her read and _____. Even though there
(present-tense verb)

are _____ of us, we sit on _____, so
(double-digit number)   (plural noun)

we are comfortable. She usually reads for _____ minutes
(double-digit number)

a day. She asked each of us to make a bookmark of our favorite book. We did

this every day for _____ days of school. Then we had
(triple-digit number)

a book fair and sold the bookmarks for _____ each to
(amount of money)

raise money for new books about _____. It was the most
(plural noun)

_____ book fair ever!
(adjective)

Solve This! How many bookmarks
did the students make? _____

Name: _____ Date: _____

Pet House

My Uncle _____
(first name of a boy)

is a builder. He builds _____
(plural noun)

out of _____. He also builds
(type of substance)

houses out of bricks. Last year he built a house for my pet

_____, _____.
(type of animal)   (first name of a boy or girl)

The house has _____ rows of bricks. Each row has
(double-digit number)

_____ bricks in it. The house has _____
(triple-digit number)   (number greater than 1)

windows and _____ doors. We painted the inside
(single-digit number greater than 1)

_____ and put _____ on the floor
(color)   (type of substance)

so it is nice and _____. My pet loves it.
(adjective)

How many bricks did the uncle
use to build the house? _____

Name: _____   Date: _____

Go, Team!

I am on a roller _____
(type of sport)

team. I love the game because it is so

_____ and _____.
(adjective)   (adjective)

Our team is called the _____ _____.
(adjective)   (plural noun)

There are _____ players on the team and we all really
(double-digit number)

needed new equipment. Each of us saved up _____
(triple-digit number)

pennies. Fortunately, that was exactly enough for each of us to get a

new _____. Now we're really ready to play the
(noun)

_____ _____. Last time we played
(name of a place)   (plural noun)

this team, we lost _____ to _____.
(triple-digit number)   (double-digit number)

That won't happen again, now that we are _____
(verb ending in -ing)

better than ever!

Solve This!   How much money did the team
spend on equipment? _____

Name: _____ Date: _____

Paying for Camp

I had to raise money so I could go to

_____ Scout Camp in
(type of animal)

_____. I love it there because we _____
(name of a place)   (present-tense verb)

and _____ all day. The air is _____
     (present-tense verb)   (adjective)

and the water is _____. I learned how to
                      (adjective)

_____ there and also how to make _____.
(present-tense verb)   (plural noun)

So you can understand how _____ it is. To pay for camp,
                               (adjective)

I decided to sell _____ that I made myself. It took
                       (plural noun)

_____ weeks to make one for each of my _____
(double-digit number)   (double-digit number)

customers. But each one paid _____ dollars and
                                  (single-digit number greater than 1)

_____ cents, and that was just enough to cover my expenses.
(double-digit number)

Now I'm on my way!

Solve This!   How much money
did the camper earn? _____

Name: _____   Date: _____

Big Diner

My Aunt _____
(first name of a girl)

owns a big diner. It's called the Golden

_____ Diner. She offered a breakfast special one day that
(noun)

only cost _____ dollars and _____
(single-digit number greater than 1)   (double-digit number)

cents. In only five hours, _____ people ordered it. Along with
(triple-digit number)

fried _____ and _____, the special
(type of food)   (type of vegetable, plural)

came with a side of _____ and a steaming cup of hot
(type of food)

_____. There was even some _____
(type of liquid)   (type of food, plural)

for dessert. That's pretty hard to beat. Everyone agreed it was really

_____!
(adjective)

Solve This! How much money did the diner
make from the breakfast special? _____

Name: _____   Date: _____

Dime Pitch

I got a new summer job at the

_____ Amusement Park where
(last name of a boy or girl)

I am in charge of the Dime Pitch game. It's very

simple and _____. Here's how it
(adjective)

works: I have _____ shelves in my stand. On each shelf
(single-digit number greater than 1)

there are _____ glasses shaped like _____.
(double-digit number)   (plural noun)

To win, you have to toss your dime into one of them. Last week,

_____ customers won _____
(triple-digit number)   (single-digit number greater than 1)

dollars and _____ cents each. I get paid
(double-digit number)

_____ dollars an hour. I spend some of it on rides like the Roller
(number greater than 1)

_____ and Flying _____.
(noun)   (plural noun)

I have a really _____ job!
(adjective)

> **Solve This!**   How much money did customers
> win at Dime Pitch last week? _____

Name: _____ Date: _____

Farm Visit

Our class went on a field trip to a nearby

_____ farm. There
　　(adjective)

were _____ of us, and
　　(double-digit even number less than 20)

we went by _____. We saw lots of
　　(mode of transportation)

_____ in the fields. We got to help feed the
　　(type of animal, plural)

_____ and brush the _____.
　　(type of animal, plural)　　　　　　　　　　　　(type of animal, plural)

We were lucky to be there when the _____ hatched their
　　　　　　　　　　　　　　　　　　　　(type of animal, plural)

eggs. The farmers here grow _____ and watermelon.
　　　　　　　　　　　　　　　(type of fruit or vegetable, plural)

There must have been _____ watermelons growing in
　　　　　　　　　　　(triple-digit number)

the field. While we were there, we each got half a watermelon for a snack. It

was so _____! I can see why everyone likes to get their
　　　(adjective)

watermelons from this farm!

Solve This!　　How many watermelons did the
farm cut in half for the class? _____

Name: _____   Date: _____

Birthday Cupcakes

I baked cupcakes with my Aunt

_____. We were making them
(first name of a girl)

for my cousin _____'s birthday.
(first name of a boy)

He is _____ years old. His favorite flavor is
(number greater than 1)

_____. We made the cupcakes really big. In
(type of flavor)

fact, they were _____ inches wide! There were
(single-digit number greater than 1)

_____ kids at the party, so we gave each one a quarter
(choose a number: 8, 12, or 16)

of a cupcake. That came out perfectly. There weren't any left over, so my aunt

and I ate _____ instead. It wasn't as good as a cupcake,
(type of food)

but it was _____!
(adjective)

Solve This! How many cupcakes
did they make? _____

Name: _____ Date: _____

The Magic Show

The Great _____-ini
(last name of a boy)

performed a magic act for our community variety

show. There were _____ of us in the audience for this
(single-digit number greater than 1)

_____ show. The magician came all the way from
(adjective)

_____, so we were _____ to see
(name of a place)   (adjective)

him. He started off with a big trick, making _____
(first name of a boy or girl)

disappear. Then he pulled _____ out of
(plural noun)

_____'s ear, and with a wave of a wand made
(first name of a boy or girl)

_____ multiply! He was really _____!
(plural noun)   (adjective)

At the end, he turned _____ into chocolate bars and gave
(plural noun)

each of us one third of a bar. It was real chocolate, and we were glad it didn't

turn into _____, or something worse!
(plural noun)

Solve This! How many chocolate bars
did the magician need? _____

Name: _____ Date: _____

Bag of Fruit

My brother, _____,
(first name of a boy)

my sister, _____, and I went to
(first name of a girl)

_____'s Fresh Fruits and Vegetables.
(last name of a boy or girl)

We looked at _____ apples, _____
(adjective)   (adjective)

bananas, and _____ oranges. We couldn't
(adjective)

decide which to get so we bought a bag of mixed fruit. There were

_____ pieces of fruit in a bag. All of the fruit was
(choose a number: 3, 6, or 9)

_____, so we just split it up evenly. We also bought
(adjective)

_____ _____ nuts. They were hard
(single-digit number greater than 1)   (name of a place)

to open so we cracked them open with my handy _____.
(type of tool)

Boy, were they _____!
(adjective)

Solve This! How many pieces of
fruit did each person get? _____

Name: _____   Date: _____

Dad's Surprise

My dad's birthday is coming up

and my brother and I bought him some

_____ presents. I got
(adjective)

him _____ _____-powered
(single-digit odd number greater than 1)   (adjective)

_____. My brother got him _____
(plural noun)   (single-digit odd number greater than 1)

cans of _____. We wrapped each item separately in
(plural noun)

_____. Then we made a cake and put
(type of substance)

_____ candles on it. We split up the presents evenly, hiding
(number greater than 1)

some in my room and some in my brother's room. When our dad finds them

all, he will be so surprised, he'll probably yell, " _____!"
(expression)

Solve This!   How many presents did
the kids hide in each room? _____

Name: _____   Date: _____

Driving to the Movies

THE END

My friends and I wanted to see that new

movie, *Return of the* _____.
                              (plural noun)

It's about this _____ who is really
                        (type of job)

a spy and has to find a missing _____. It is totally
                                         (noun)

_____. There were a dozen of us kids going and
        (adjective)

_____ parents driving. We split up evenly, got in
(choose a number: 2, 3, 4, or 6)

the cars, and got to the movie theater right on time. We bought some

_____ and _____ from the
      (type of food)   (type of food)

snack bar and found seats. The movie was _____
                                                (triple-digit number)

minutes long. My friend _____ fell asleep and started
                           (first name of a boy or girl)

_____. That was a little _____.
   (verb ending in -ing)   (adjective)

Solve This! How many kids
went in each car? _____

Name: _____ Date: _____

Time for a Snack

I love snacks. My mother always

packs me things like chocolate-covered

_____ and sour _____ .
(plural noun)   (plural noun)

The other day she gave me a bag of _____ -coated
(type of food)

crackers. There were _____ crackers in the bag. I wanted
(choose a number: 12, 16, or 20)

to share them equally with three of my friends, _____ ,
(first name of a boy or girl)

_____ , and _____ . The crackers
(first name of a boy or girl)   (name of a famous person)

were so _____ , we ate them all in _____
(adjective)   (number greater than 1)

seconds. We finished up with some _____ -flavored
(type of food)

soda to drink. Next time, my mom says she'll pack a bag of gummy

_____ . My friends can't wait!
(plural noun)

Solve This! How many crackers
did each person get? _____

Name: _____ Date: _____

Land Rush!

Good news for all space explorers! There was a

land rush on Planet _____.
(name of a famous person)

The space explorers from _____ were the first to
(name of a place)

arrive. They jetted there in the Starship _____
(adjective)

_____. There were _____ explorers
(noun) (number from 2 to 9)

in the group, not counting Starship Commander _____.
(last name of a boy or girl)

The explorers found _____ acres of land, claimed
(any double-digit number)

them all, and shared them equally. The Starship Commander did not get any

land. He was happy just to collect _____ specimens
(noun)

while he was there. There were also rare _____
(color)

_____ and rivers that flowed with _____.
(plural noun) (type of liquid)

That planet is quite a place!

Solve This! How much land did each explorer get? _____
Use the back of the page to explain your answer.

Name: _____   Date: _____

Pizza Time

_____ makes the best pizza.
(first and last name of a girl)

It is more _____ and
(adjective)

_____ than any other pizza.
(adjective)

She makes it with lots of _____ and melted
(type of food)

_____, and bakes it in her _____.
(type of food)   (noun)

It's always _____ and _____ when
(adjective)   (adjective)

it comes out of the oven. Last week she made _____
(double-digit number)

pizzas and distributed them equally to the lucky _____
(single-digit number greater than 1)

players on the _____ball team. The players were so
(noun)

_____, they made her a card that said, "You are the
(adjective)

_____ friend ever!"
(adjective ending in -est)

Solve This! How many pizzas did each player get? _____

Name: _____   Date: _____

Plant Experiment

D r. _____ of the
        (first and last name of a girl)

_____ Plant Project has been
(name of a place)

growing _____ plants for _____ years.
           (noun)   (number greater than 1)

She wondered if plants would grow better with a liquid other than water.

She tested _____ and _____ and
           (type of liquid)   (type of liquid)

found that both made the plants _____. She finally
                      (adjective)

tried _____, which she called Liquid X. She distributed
     (type of liquid)

_____ ounces of Liquid X evenly among _____
(double-digit number)   (single-digit number greater than 1)

plants. The plants immediately became _____ and grew
                       (adjective)

_____ inches in only _____ hours. The results
(number greater than 1)   (number greater than 1)

were truly _____!
           (adjective)

Solve This! How many ounces of Liquid X did each plant get? _____

50 Fill-In Math Word Problems: Multiplication & Division: Grades 4–6 © 2009 by Bob Krech and Joan Novelli, Scholastic Teaching Resources

Name: _____   Date: _____

Raising Money

My friends _____,
(first name of a boy or girl)

_____, and _____
(first name of a boy or girl)   (name of a famous person)

and I wanted to earn some money. I wanted to make enough to buy a new

_____. After lots of discussion, we decided to set up a
(noun)

stand to sell _____. We figured people would really like
(type of liquid)

a drink of that on those _____ days. We charged only
(adjective)

one cent for a cup. We sold _____ cups. All of our
(choose a number: 40, 80, 160, or 320)

customers said it was the most _____ drink they'd ever
(adjective)

had. We divided the money evenly among us. Next time I think we will also

sell _____ to eat along with the drink. Then I think
(plural noun)

our sales will be so _____, I will earn enough to buy a
(adjective)

new _____!
(noun)

Solve This! How much money
did each person make? _____

Name: _____ Date: _____

Alien Visit

_____ recently hosted
(first and last name of a girl)

visitors from Planet _____.
(last name of a boy or girl)

She admired their very cool _____
(plural noun)

and their wonderful _____ _____.
(color)   (plural noun)

She met five aliens in all. She wanted to give them each a welcoming gift,

so she bought a box of _____ computer programs
(double-digit number ending in 5 or 0)

and gave an equal number to each alien. The aliens were so grateful

they gave her _____ _____
(single-digit number greater than 1)   (adjective)

_____ as a thank-you gift. I bet she can't wait for
(plural noun)

them to come back again!

Solve This! How many computer programs
did each alien get? _____

Name: _____   Date: _____

Train Ride

I am taking the train to visit my grandmother.

She lives in _____ and is
                    (name of a place)

_____ years old. The trip is _____
(double-digit number greater than 30)   (single-digit number greater than 1)

hours long, and we will pass through _____ and
                                            (name of a place)

_____. I brought a bag of _____
       (name of a place)   (adjective)

pretzels in case I get hungry. There are _____ pretzels in the
                                               (double-digit number)

bag. I'm going to eat the same number of pretzels each hour of the trip

so I can be sure they will last the whole trip. Any leftovers I'll save for the

way back! I also brought a great book to read. It's called *The Autobiography*

of _____. One reviewer said, "This book is so
       (name of a famous person)

_____, I couldn't put it down." It sounds like just the
         (adjective)

kind of book I like to _____.
                          (present-tense verb)

Solve This!

What's the greatest number of pretzels
the train traveler can eat each hour? _____
Will there be any pretzels for
the way back? If so, how many? _____

Name: _____   Date: _____

Don't Miss the Tour

My dad started a family business. We run a

tour company. We take people to see famous places

like _____'s Mountain or the
        (last name of a boy or girl)

_____ River. We just had our most popular tour ever.
        (last name of a boy or girl)

We took our guests to see _____'s house. Yes, it was
                                (name of a famous person)

the actual house! We advertised the tour and charged _____
                                                            (number greater than 1)

dollars per person. A thousand people showed up! We divided the group

evenly and put everyone on _____ buses. We
                                (choose a number: 2, 4, 5, or 8)

gave each guest a souvenir _____ and a map. The
                                        (noun)

tour lasted _____ hours. People said it was the
                (single-digit number greater than 1)

_____ tour ever!
        (adjective ending in -est)

Solve This!   How many people
rode on each bus? _____

Name: _____   Date: _____

New Coach

We have a new coach for our

_____ team. Her name is
(name of a sport)

_____. She is very tough, but also _____.
(first and last name of a girl)   (adjective)

To get ready for the season, we have to run _____
                                              (number greater than 1)

miles every day and do _____ pushups. We also have
                          (number greater than 1)

to swim 2,500 laps in the pool. At least we get to split up the swimming

evenly over _____ days. For team spirit, we all
              (choose a number: 2, 4, or 5)

wear _____ _____ to school.
        (color)   (article of clothing)

And every chance we get, we sing our team song, "You Make Me Want

to _____." This is going to be a very interesting and
    (verb)

_____ season.
    (adjective)

Solve This! How many laps does the
team have to swim each day? _____

Name: _____   Date: _____

Book Drive

Our class organized a book drive. We collected

5,000 books in _____ days.
(number greater than 1)

Our teacher couldn't believe how many _____ books we
(adjective)

collected. People donated books like *The Story of* _____,
(plural noun)

by _____ and *How to* _____,
(first and last name of a boy or girl)   (present-tense verb)

by _____. Some books were
(name of a famous person)

_____ and other books were just _____.
(adjective)   (adjective)

As books came in, we organized them in _____.
(type of container, plural)

Then we divided up the books evenly and donated them to

_____ schools. To thank us for our good work, our
(choose a number: 2, 4, 5, or 8)

teacher gave everyone in the class a new _____.
(noun)

That made us feel so _____!
(adjective)

Solve This! How many books did the
class donate to each school? _____

Division With Single-Digit Divisor and Four-Digit Dividend

Treasure Hunt

Captain Jack _____ and
(last name of a boy)

his pirate crew found a treasure map. The treasure appeared to be located on

the Island of _____. So they set sail on their ship, the
(last name of a boy or girl)

_____ _____. After hunting for
(adjective)   (noun)

_____ days, they finally discovered the treasure chest. Inside,
(number greater than 1)

they found _____ _____! They divided the
(four-digit number)   (plural noun)

treasure evenly among the crew of _____ and Captain
(single-digit number greater than 1)

Jack. As always, Captain Jack claimed any extra. Then they celebrated by

roasting _____ over an open fire and singing a celebration
(type of food, plural)

song, "You've Got to Be _____." What an amazingly
(adjective)

_____ adventure!
(adjective)

Solve This!

How much treasure did
each member pirate get? _____

Does Captain Jack get
anything extra? If so, how much? _____

Division With Single-Digit Divisor and Four-Digit Dividend

Homework!

Our new teacher, Mr. _____,

(last name of a famous man)

loves to assign homework. He says it makes us

_____ and _____. I think he is

(adjective)   (adjective)

_____. He is especially _____ when it

(adjective)   (adjective)

comes to rules. We have to do all our writing with _____

(plural noun)

and we can't even use our _____. He just gave us

(noun)

_____ pages of math problems to do over vacation! I am

(four-digit number)

going to split up the assignment evenly over _____ days.

(single-digit number greater than 1)

Any remaining page I am going to have my _____ sister do. Even so, it

(age)

makes me want to _____ my _____.

(present-tense verb)   (noun)

Solve This!

How many pages of math problems
must be done each day? _____

How many pages will the sister do? _____

Class Contest

My class entered a contest. Our teacher,

Ms. _____, thought it would
(last name of a famous female)

be _____ for us. The contest was simple:
(adjective)

We had to throw one _____ at an ordinary
(noun)

_____-shaped target. All _____
(noun)   (choose a number: 15, 20, or 25)

students took a turn and all together, we scored _____ points,
(triple-digit number)

which put our class in _____ place! Our teacher, of
(ordinal number)

course, was very _____ with our performance, and said
(adjective)

"_____!" We won _____ dollars
(exclamation)   (choose a number: 100, 200, or 250)

that we will share evenly. I was so _____,
(adjective)

I _____ all day!
(verb ending in -ed)

Solve This!

How much money
will each student get? _____

Name: _____ Date: _____

Birthday Money

I just turned _____ years
(number greater than 1)

old. On my birthday I got a brand-new _____
(noun)

and a cool _____ with wheels. I also got
(noun)

_____ dollars from my Uncle _____.
(triple-digit number) _(first name of a boy)_

Because my brother, _____, and my sister,
(first name of a boy)

_____, are so sneaky, I am going to hide the money equally
(first name of a girl)

in _____ places. Any extra I will put in the bank. I will take out
(double-digit number)

a little bit each week to buy things, like my favorite _____ or
(noun)

a special _____ set of _____. I will also
(adjective) _(plural noun)_

save some of the money so I can go to _____ University. I
(last name of a boy or girl)

want to study to become a fine _____, just like my uncle!
(type of occupation)

What's the most money that could
go equally into each hiding place? _____

How much will go in the bank? _____

Name: _____   Date: _____

Halloween Party

W e had a really _____
_____(adjective)

Halloween party at my house this year. We put

_____ streamers all over everything. We carved
_____(color)

_____ and put candles in them. We even had some fake
___(type of food, plural)

black _____. There were _____
_____(type of animal, plural)   _____(choose a number: 10, 25, or 50)

guests. We played Bobbing for _____ and
_____(type of fruit, plural)

Musical _____. I dressed up as a really
_____(plural noun)

_____ _____, and my sister's
_____(adjective)   _____(noun)

costume made her look just like _____. For treats, we
_____(name of a famous person)

gave out 1,000 chocolate-covered _____. Each guest got
_____(plural noun)

the same number. Everyone said it was the most _____
_____(adjective)

party ever!

Solve This!   How many treats
did each guest get? _____

Division With Double-Digit Divisor and Four-Digit Dividend

The Long Book

The _____ writer,
(adjective)

Mr. _____, just finished his
(first and last name of a boy)

newest book, *The Story of the* _____
(adjective)

_____. It is expected to sell _____
(plural noun)   (number greater than 1)

copies overnight! The cover has a picture of two _____
(plural noun)

_____. That will certainly catch the reader's
(verb ending in -ing)

_____. The book is a whopping _____
(body part)   (choose a number: 2,000, 4,000, or 5,000)

pages, which the author divided evenly into _____
(choose a number: 10, 20, 25, 40, or 50)

chapters. The first chapter is called "The _____." That will
(plural noun)

get people interested in reading it right away. And it only costs _____!
(amount of money)

This book is definitely a bargain.

Solve This! How many pages are in
each chapter of the book? _____

Name: _____ Date: _____

Contest Winners

Our class just won third place in a big contest

sponsored by _____.
(name of a company)

We had to write an essay called "My Favorite _____."
(noun)

We worked in groups to write each paragraph, and we took turns

_____ the essay before turning it in. First
(verb ending in -ing)

prize was a gold _____. Second prize was an
(noun)

electronic _____. Third prize was a pack of
(noun)

_____ stickers. We have _____
(four-digit number)   (two-digit number less than 30)

students in our class and we are going to share the stickers as evenly as

possible. Any extras we will give to our teacher. We also got a letter from

_____ congratulating us and saying that we are a
(name of a famous person)

really _____ class!
(adjective)

Solve This!

How many stickers should each student get? _____

How many stickers will the teacher get? _____

Name: _____   Date: _____

Class Pets

Mr. _____ is a
(last name of a boy)

really _____ teacher.
(adjective)

He always lets his students have class pets. We used to have

_____, but that didn't work out. They were too
(type of animal, plural)

_____ and they kept _____.
(adjective)   (verb ending in -ing)

Now we have goldfish. In fact, we have _____ of them! Summer
(four-digit number)

vacation is almost here, so we decided to divide up the goldfish so we

could all help take care of them. There are _____ students in
(two-digit number)

our class and everyone wants as many fish as possible. We'll divide up

the fish equally, and give our teacher any extras to take home. We will

have to feed them _____ every day, and keep their
(type of food)

_____ clean.
(type of liquid)

Solve This!
How many goldfish will each student get? _____

How many will the teacher take home? _____

Name: _____ Date: _____

Building a Tower

I, Sir _____-a-Lot,
(present-tense verb)

a Knight of the Kingdom of _____, was asked by Queen
(last name of a boy or girl)

_____ to build her a tower. She, of course, is the most
(first name of a girl)

_____ queen in all the land. This tower was to keep
(adjective)

her safe from her wicked step-_____, so she wanted it to
(noun)

be _____ feet high. I was given _____ days to do it. I
(four-digit number)   (double-digit number)

will break up the job, building an equal number of feet each day. If there is

extra to be done, I will have my loyal friend, Sir _____
(first name of a boy)

the _____take care of that for me. It is going to be a
(adjective)

lot of _____ work, but the queen has promised me
(adjective)

_____ golden _____ when I am finished!
(number greater than 1)   (plural noun)

Solve This!

How many feet of the tower should the
knight build each day? _____

How many feet will the loyal
friend have to build? _____

Dividing Simple Fractions

The Pie

My Aunt _____ is an
(first name of a girl)

especially _____ cook.
(adjective)

She works at that famous restaurant, The Old

_____ Inn. Her specialties are roast
(adjective)

_____ and fried _____, and people
(noun)   (noun)

come from as far away as _____ for it. She also makes
(name of a place)

the best _____ pie. She gave _____
(noun)   (choose a number: 1, 3, or 5)

of my friends and me half of a pie, which we split between us evenly. It

had a little _____ sprinkled on top and I added some
(noun)

_____ to my piece for extra flavor. It tasted completely
(type of substance)

_____.
(adjective)

Solve This!   What part of the whole
pie did each person get? _____

Name: _____ Date: _____

Dividing Simple Fractions

Wood Shop Class

Here at _____
(last name of a teacher)

Elementary School we have Wood Shop Class.

Ms. _____ is our teacher. She is very
(last name of a girl)

_____, but still fun. For our first project, we had
(adjective)

to make _____ out of wood. They weren't very
(plural noun)

_____ but they were good for _____. Now
(adjective)   (verb ending in -ing)

we are making _____ out of wood. For this project, our
(plural noun)

teacher cut up a big sheet of plywood. She gave my group one fourth of it to

divide evenly among the _____ people in our group. Now I need
(choose a number: 2 or 4)

to use my _____ and my _____ to
(type of tool)   (type of tool)

get to work on it. I figure it will only take _____ days. When
(number greater than 1)

mine is finished, I can use it to _____.
(present-tense verb)

Solve This! What portion of the plywood
did each group member get? _____

Dividing Simple Fractions

Discovery!

Our fearless leader, _____, recently took
(name of a famous man)

_____ of us cave explorers on an expedition. We went to the
(choose a number: 2 or 3)

Caves of _____ in _____. We
(last name of a boy or girl)   (name of a place)

were about _____ feet below the surface, in a cave called Old
(number greater than 1)

_____. We had our equipment, including lamps, helmets,
(adjective)

_____, and _____. As we got deeper
(plural noun)   (plural noun)

into the cave, we saw something _____. We dug there and
(adjective)

found a great _____ made of solid gold! We brought it to the
(noun)

surface and discussed what we should do with it. Our leader kept two thirds for

himself, and said that we could split the rest equally. I am going to buy a new

_____ with my share. Our fearless leader used his to buy the
(noun)

_____ he had been wanting, which he is wearing right now!
(noun)

Solve This!

What part of the gold
did each explorer get? _____

50 Fill-In Math Word Problems: Multiplication & Division: Grades 4–6 © 2009 by Bob Krech and Joan Novelli, Scholastic Teaching Resources